David J. König

Sports Betting Instead of Stocks!

9 Steps to Passive Income Through Sports Betting! How to Find Serious Tipsters and Successfully Invest in the Sports Betting Market

Inhaltsverzeichnis

Introductory Remarks

"It's not gambling, if you know,

that you will win in the long run!"

Do you want to change your life and become a professional in sports betting? Do you want to achieve this in a short time? Do you want to earn money by following the best betting experts in the world? Would you like to earn far higher returns than are possible with conventional forms of investment such as stocks, investment funds and real estate? Then this is the book for you. Here I teach you a comprehensive basic knowledge of sports betting and give you a method of how to invest in the sports betting market without taking unnecessary risks and without sitting up on scammers.

First, however, we must clear up a misconception that you may also limit yourself with. I'll give you some advice: Tell only selected people that you're investing in sports betting - it's best not to tell everyone. Why? Sports betting has a bad image. For many people it is a useless pastime for stupid people who don't realize that they are being ripped off by bookmakers and betting offices. Most are of the rock-solid conviction that one gambles his money in the long run with sport bets. "In the end, it's always the bank that wins," is a well-known wise saying. But this only applies to those sports bettors who don't know what they are doing. People who think they know better than the bookmakers who will win the final of the Champions League. These poor people have no idea what the odds offered by the bookmakers really say (more about that later).

But just as unfortunate are the ignorant people who don't realize what potential the sports betting market has and how much money they are losing by not participating in the profits from sports betting. These people have false beliefs. But let these people continue to put their money on their savings books at the local savings bank and make do with 0.1 percent interest.

Instead, remember the following sentence: "It's not gambling if you know you'll win in the long run". If you know that your own betting strategy gives you an advantage over the bookmakers, then you can prove mathematically that you will make juicy profits in the long run and it is no longer a game of chance. Happiness only determines success in the short term, ability only in the long term.

There are professional sports bettors who can live of the betting business without any problems, and some have even become multimillionaires (such a successful person is introduced in Chapter 1). But it is an incredibly difficult business that requires years of experience, specialist knowledge and a constant willingness to adapt to the changing sports betting markets.

There are sports bettors who have been professionally active in sports for years and who have developed a feeling for the probability distribution with which possible outcomes can be evaluated. And then there are the mathematically versed sports bettors, who can evaluate extensive statistical material for a game and thus calculate a certain probability for a game event based on data. If these sports bettors see that a bookmaker underestimates the probability for a certain outcome of a game, they bet on this event. Some bets get lost - that's the calculated risk - but in the long run, this results in high returns.

But to make it to this level takes a lot of time and effort. It takes years of work on your own betting models; you must learn a lot without knowing whether one day you will actually manage to become a profitable sports bettor.

But what if you could follow the tips of the profitable sports bettor and get a big piece of the cake? If you didn't have to go the rocky road to become a sports betting millionaire? How do you find such serious providers of sports betting tips? The problem: Each of us knows corresponding advertisements: "Follow these tips and you make crass profits for just so and so much euros a month", "Come to our Facebook/WhatsApp group and become the sports betting king with us! Most of these providers are "rat catchers"! These are simple scams. This book will show you how to filter out the serious sports bettor.

Now you will ask why a sports bettor should sell its tips, if it supposedly earns so much money with it itself. The answer is simple: Selling tips that you have played yourself will give you a regular income in addition to the sports betting winnings without negatively affecting your own sports betting business. In this way, he can continue to build up his betting bank (the sum of money available for betting) and bet more money in the future. So why shouldn't a profitable sports better sell his tips? It's a win-win situation for tip sellers and tip buyers.

Before you jump to the next chapter, I would like to summarize three advantages of sports betting over other ways of making money, so that you can realize the full potential of the knowledge contained in this book.

Advantage No. 1: With Sports Betting You Can Generate a Passive Income

Most people earn their money in this way: their alarm clock rings at seven in the morning, then they have breakfast and go to work. They stay there until the evening. For this they receive a salary and thus earn an active income. The opposite is passive income. This means that you earn money even when you are not working. Now you no longer exchange your valuable time for money, as with active income, but you separate your working time from your income. The product or service that you offer or the form of investment in which you invest your money therefore works without your own involvement. The following prerequisites must be met: firstly, low maintenance and updating costs and secondly, a high degree of automation of your business model.

However, a certain amount of work is necessary to achieve this goal. In our case, you must invest some time in reading this book, acquire the knowledge, internalize it and then implement the advice.

In general, there are several ways to generate a passive income. One is renting a flat or a room. Here you receive monthly rent as a passive income without having to invest a lot of time in the long run. It is just as lucrative to rent your own car, if it is unused for a large part of the time and even consumes money in the form of tax and insurance. If you have a passion for a particular subject, I would recommend that you create and sell online courses or webinars. Once you've built this digital product, selling it takes little time. You can also write about your hobby on your own website and include affiliate links. When a person clicks on such a link, they will be redirected to your affiliate site, e.g. amazon.com. If the person buys the referred product, you receive a commission, a share of the sales value.

The easiest way to earn passive income is to invest part of your active income profitably. First you think of government bonds, stocks, investment funds or ETFs (exchange-traded funds), but the investment in sports betting offers much more chances of profit. And this brings us to the second advantage of sports betting.

Advantage No. 2: Sports Betting Is More Lucrative Than Most Other Financial Products

If you simply want to store your assets as securely as possible, then of course a call money account, a savings book or government bonds are the better choice. But if you want to make more out of your money and invest it with a significant profit, then you will quickly come to the topic of stocks and other financial products. By buying a share you profit from two things: On the one hand from the dividend, i.e. the annual distribution of the company to the shareholders or shareholders, and on the other hand (hopefully) from any price gains. The latter means that your stock will increase in value and you could sell it at a profit. However, you will only make price gains if the stock rises in value. Dividends are usually paid out only once a year and then often do not amount to more than about 2-3 percent - if a dividend is paid at all. Even dividend-oriented investment funds often offer no more than an annual return of no more than 5 percent.

The massive advantage of sports betting is as follows: In contrast to dividend payments through shares, sports betting can generate profits not only annually, but MONTHLY and these profits are considerably higher than with conventional financial products. You can generate a monthly return rate of 5-10 percent without much effort, i.e. you can post 5-10 cents as profit for every euro you set in the month. In other words: If you bet 10,000 EUR in one month (distributed over a multitude of bets), you can book 500-1,000 EUR of it as profit.

However, you must be aware of one thing. An old financial wisdom is, "the higher the winnings, the higher the risk". It can also happen that you lose several bets in a row despite good tips. However, these unlucky streaks are considered in our risk management and are no cause for concern. For us only the long-term profit counts!

Whether this is to be expected can be checked with the method presented in this book flawlessly.

Advantage No. 3: Your Capital Is Only Tied Up for a Short Time

If you invest your money in shares, then this capital is tied up until the share is sold. Some investment funds, especially real estate funds, even have a holding period, i.e. you are not allowed to sell your purchased fund shares for a certain period after the purchase, e.g. two years.

If you need the invested money unexpectedly, then you must sell shares - often with a price loss, of course, because you can't wait for a better time to sell. In the case of government bonds or the funds mentioned, you won't even get your money.

Sports betting is different. With every bet, you bet a small part of your betting bank, i.e. of all the capital you have available for betting. Depending on how many tips you buy from serious betting experts to re-type, you can even bet your betting bank several times. This means that you have a high cash flow rate, i.e. you can turn over a lot of money in a short period of time at a manageable risk and generate correspondingly high winnings - on average, you receive a certain percentage of winnings for every bet you make. So, at any given time, only a small percentage of your capital is tied up and only for as long as the bet runs. If you bet in the morning on a game that takes place in the evening, then this capital, including the win, is available again after the game - if the bet has been won. This money will be back in your account within a short time and will be available for you to invest again.

After explaining the obvious advantages of understanding sports betting as an investment, I'll start with the ten-step plan below. The first step should help you to finally break up with the wrong belief that sports betting is not profitable in the long run. In the second step, I will teach you the basic knowledge of the topic, what types of bets there are, and so on. In the third step I will introduce you to the holy grail of sports betting: The value betting, called value betting in German. Value betting is what successful sports bets do. You only choose bets that have a positive expectation value and thus promise a positive profit expectation - but more about that later.

In the fourth step, we want to understand how the bookmakers work. Step five is the core of the book: In this section I finally explain how you can distinguish successful betting tip providers from dubious sellers and how you can control whether your purchased bets have a positive profit expectation.

In step six, I'll explain everything about diversifying your tipster portfolio. You may already know diversification from the stock market. It is recommended there to diversify your investments as widely as possible, figuratively speaking not only to bet on one horse in order to reduce the overall risk.

In the seventh step, I explain how and to whom you can place your bets. In step eight I remind you that it is important for a passive income not to invest too much time - otherwise it would be an active income because you exchange time for money again. That's why this chapter explains how you can automate betting with software. In the ninth and final step, I want to warn you against being too greedy. Instead, I'll show you a way to use your capital wisely and minimize the risk.

Step 1: Convince Yourself: Joachim Marnitz. An Example of a Rreal Sports Betting Millionaire

In the introduction I spoke of professional sports bettors who have gone the long rocky road until they have finally managed to bet profitably. This is the typical painful, but also exciting way of any professional bettor. We want to profit from such successful sports betting experts.

To help you convince yourself that it is actually possible to build up a fortune with sports betting, I would like to introduce an authentic sports betting millionaire in this chapter:

His name is Joachim Marnitz and I learned a lot from him about the sports betting business. He became a millionaire through his bets and gained financial freedom. He could now relax all year round on a Southesse island, but he is still busy with his passion - sports betting.

The first question that comes to mind is, of course, how he managed to be so successful in the betting business. The basis for his betting success is the knowledge he acquired during his studies. He studied sociology to a diploma. The focus was on empirical social research and thus on the field of statistics. Exactly this forms the basis of his successful competitive career. He says this in an interview:

"You can't compare that with the beer bet on the weekend. Before a bet I analyze numerous data sets, the odds movements for both teams in the past as well as the special conditions of the game. For example, whether certain players are banned or injured."

The path to professional bettor is always the same: you develop a method and constantly refine it. His ambition was to see the whole thing as a mathematical challenge. There have also been difficult periods in which several bets have been lost and he has slipped into the red, but he has the right answer for himself:

"It's like successful poker players. Luck and bad luck only play an important role in the meantime. In the long run, skill is the deciding factor."

Marnitz compares professional betting with stock trading. With the share purchase it is the goal to buy and again sell undervalued shares if they are overvalued. The same thing is done when betting: You bet on game events whose probability is wrongly evaluated by the bookmakers and thus receive a positive profit expectation (but more on this later).

The average working day at Marnitz is as follows: He invests a lot of time in the development and improvement of his betting models. He is also concerned with obtaining statistical data on the games as efficiently as possible and analyzing his daily bets. When he finds lucrative bets, he bets on them. He scans market developments with a computer program that makes his work much easier:

"The actual analysis of a single bet therefore does not take so long. However, there is a lot of work involved in the development of the underlying model."

Active work as a sports betting professional therefore requires a lot of time and know-how. It is therefore much easier to buy repayable bets from professional tipsters!

Nevertheless, as tip buyers, we should also familiarize ourselves with the basics of the matter. Marnitz recommends that everyone familiarize themselves with betting theory.

(The basis for these chapters was personal correspondence between the author and Marnitz and an online interview on hochgepokert.com, conducted by Goran: *"Joachim Marnitz - Ein Sportwetten-Millionär im Interview"*).

Step 2: Learn the Basics: Concepts and Basic Terminology

This chapter explains the basics of sports betting. Let's be stupid: What are sports bets anyway? It's very simple: As with any other bet, bets are placed on the occurrence of a certain event, such as the victory of a certain team with a financial stake. If you lose the bet, then of course you also lose your stake. However, if you bet on the right event, your winnings will be measured by the odds you bet on.

The Odds

In the European system, the quota is expressed as a decimal number. The odds are the value by which your bet is multiplied in the event of a win, i.e. when your bet pays off. Let's take as an example a match from the German Bundesliga:

Vfl Wolfsburg vs. Werder Bremen

Here a bookmaker offers the following odds on the popular bet on home win, draw or away win:

Vfl Wolfsburg home win: 2.28

Tie: 3.52

Away win Werder Bremen: 3.31

At this match we now bet that the home team will win and bet on this event 100 euros. Should Vfl Wolfsburg win, then our stake of 100 Euro will be multiplied by the odds of 2,28. This results in the following calculation:

100 Euro (bet) x 2.28 (odds) = 228 Euro win

The bookmaker would therefore pay you the sum of 228 euros, i.e. credit it to your betting account. However, this is the gross profit. Your bet will also be refunded.

Therefore, you subtract your stake from the calculated 228 Euro of 100 Euro. Consequently, you can book 128 Euro as net profit.

Surely you are now wondering why different odds were offered on different events. This is because the odds embody assumed probabilities. For an event that is very likely to happen (e.g. a victory for FC Bayern Munich), the bookmakers only offer small odds (usually less than 1.25). Otherwise, the bookmakers would have to pay out immense sums in the event of a very probable event and they would quickly go bankrupt. The bookmakers have experts who calculate the probability of the various events based on game statistics, information about injuries, game positions, etc. The bookmakers are also able to calculate the probability of the various events. This results in the odds. Odds can be converted into their implied probabilities. It is quite simple: divide 100 by the decimal quota:

In our example, the odds for a victory of Vfl Wolfsburg were 2.28, therefore:

$$100: 2.28=44 \text{ \% (rounded)}$$

The probability of occurrence calculated by the bookmakers for the match event was thus 44 %. Statistically speaking, the bookmakers theoretically assume that Vfl Wolfsburg would win 44 out of 100 matches like this one.

The so-called "fair odds", however, would be a little higher, since the bookmakers still deduct a certain margin, so that the odds would be somewhat lower. We must consider this, but it is not an obstacle for our weather success. The aim is to only place bets whose odds, minus the margin, nevertheless promise a positive expected value. This is where professional sports bettors can benefit from the fact that bookmakers not only set the odds according to the calculated probability distribution, but also according to the assumed betting behavior of their customers. Odds for favorites and well-known club or player names, on which many fun bets rely, are therefore often set too low, while outsiders are sometimes overestimated.

The Bet Types

Head-to-head betting

The example above is a bet on the outcome of the game, which is the most popular bet - victory, defeat or, in football, a draw. Therefore, this is called a three-way bet (short: 1x2). Ice hockey is another sport that also has three possible outcomes.

In most sports, however, there are only two possible outcomes. This is called head-to-head betting (H2H for short). In sports such as tennis, basketball or baseball, you can only bet on the victory of one of the two opponents, a draw is not possible. If in the American basketball league NBA, the New York Knicks play against the Chicago Bulls, then either the Knicks or the Bulls win. A draw is not possible.

The H2H principle has also been applied to football. Here, many bookmakers also offer such bets, if a draw is played, then the bet gets its stake back. But the odds are lower. So, beware: Contrary to a widespread opinion, the probability of betting correctly in a two-way bet is not higher than in a three-way bet, since the odds offered include the different probabilities.

Over/Under Bets

Over/Under bets are usually bets on the points or goals scored in a match. Let's take the above examples. In a football match between Vfl Wolfsburg and Werder Bremen you could bet on the total number of goals scored. You can typically bet on this for the entire season in the scale above/below 0.5/1.5/2.5/3.5/4.5. If you bet on goals below 0.5, then you have won if it is 0:0 at the final whistle. If it is 1:0 or higher at the end, then you have lost. If you bet over 1.5, you must score more than two goals to win, if you bet 2.5, you must score more than three and so on. But you can only bet on the score of the first or second half, e.g. first half under 1.5 goals, i.e. not more than one goal may fall in the first half of the game.

Both to score is a type of bet where you must indicate whether you expect both teams to score or not. You can also bet on specific scores (0:0, 1:0, 0:1, 2:0, etc.). Both last mentioned bet types are rarely seen with professionals, because they are difficult to predict and therefore the over/under is preferred.

Handicap bets

With handicap bets, you give an advantage or disadvantage to one of the teams or players of a game by adding or subtracting some points or goals.

Let us first turn to the so-called European Handicap (short: EH) and illustrate the principle with the following example: Quotas for a victory of FC Bayern Munich are often set very low, if the Bavarians play against a team from the lower half of the table. Of course, this is because of the high probability that the Bavarians will sweep the opponent team off the pitch and win the game. The odds are usually in the range of less than 1.25 (remember again: The odds of 1.25 means that you would get 25 net winnings if you bet 100 Euro in case of a win. The converted probability, which implies the odds, is 80%, namely 100 divided by 1.25. The bookmaker therefore considers the event very probable). If you assume that the Bavarians will win with more than one goal gap, you can make a handicap bet and deduct one, two or more goals from the team. Accordingly, the odds offered are higher and more lucrative. Let's suppose you bet on a European handicap 0:1 with the victory of Bavaria in an away game. This means that you give the opponent team of FC Bayern a goal advantage. For the bet to work, the Bavarians must win by at least two goals, e.g. 0:2 or 1:3. If they only play 1:1 or 0:1, then after deducting the -1 goal from the final result, both teams have a tie, a draw and you have lost the bet. By the way, the European handicap is a three-way bet. You can also bet on a draw.

This is different with the Asian handicap (short: AH). These are two-way bets. Professionals prefer the Asian handicap. Let's stick to the example of the Bavarians. An AH -1 means that a goal is deducted from the Bavarians again. Unlike the EH -1, however, you do not lose the bet if the goal is equal after it has been deducted from the final result. If the score is 0:1, the result after deduction of the negative goal is 0:0 and you did not win the bet, but you did not lose it. It will be cancelled, and you will get your stake back.

Besides the Asian handicaps with whole goals, there is also the gradation with half steps and quarter steps. If the Asian handicap is -0.5 on the victory of the Bavarians, only half a goal will be deducted. If they win 0:1, you win half of the bet, the rest of the bet is refunded without a win. The same with an Asian handicap -0.25. If the Bavarians win 0:1, then you have won 75% of the bet, a quarter of the bet will be refunded. These gradations serve to adjust the betting risk and are always worth considering.

Combination bets

Combined bets belong to the realm of the fun bettor, but are also used by professionals and should therefore be discussed here. You can combine as many bets as you like with many bookmakers. Triple combos are popular. This bet type is so popular among fun bettors because the combination multiplies the odds. Let's take the following example:

You take three games on your betting slip and bet on the victory of each team in the 1x2 betting market:

Victory Vfl Wolfsburg at odds of 2.28

Victory of RB Leipzig at a quota of 3,0

Victory of Hertha BSC at a rate of 2.5

The odds are multiplied, resulting in a final odd of 17.1. Your bet would be offset against an extremely high odds, but the probability that the bet will be won is correspondingly low. The odds are only 6%. All bets must be won for this betting slip to open! If you lose one of the bets, the slip is nullified.

This is why it is so important to understand the significance of the odds and to know that they imply probabilities. The higher the odds, the less likely a win is. Therefore, amateurs primarily abandon combination bets in the betting business who have big dreams but little sense of probability. Then you had better play the lottery, it's less nerve-racking.

Professionals also use combination bets from time to time, but then mostly only double bets, i.e. two bets on one ticket and this usually only to increase very small odds through multiplication. If the odds are very low, you would otherwise have to choose a high stake in order to achieve the target win. This requires an undesirable high stake. Instead of double bets, this problem can also be solved with the handicap bets described above.

Note: Professional tipsters usually only offer single bets!

Step 3: Advance to the Core of Professional Sports Betting: Value Betting

What is the difference between an amateur, fun bettor and a real professional sports bettor that makes a big profit? What makes these professionals different? The answer is: they are not looking for the winners of a game, but for inefficient prizes, for wrongly set odds, so-called value bets. It's like trading stocks. Shares are bought if they are undervalued and therefore it can be assumed that they will rise in price and sold again if they are overvalued by the market.

The odds also fluctuate strongly until the beginning of a game. The opening odds rarely correspond to the closing odds, i.e. the last odds offered before the game begins. After the bookmakers have published their odds, they begin to fluctuate. With every new information that flows into the market, the odds are adjusted. If, for example, the injury of a key player becomes known, this will have a significant effect on the odds. But the money itself, which has already been bet on the respective game, is regarded as information. Nobody would bet 10,000 EUR (yes, such sums are played by professionals) if he did not have significant knowledge that he is getting better odds than the true probability. The Efficient Market Hypothesis says that the big bets involve knowledge and bring the market into balance. By exploiting his edge, he makes the market more efficient. The money flows thus correspond to a flow of information to which the quota markets react, the bookmakers adjust the quotas until the market is back where it should be according to true probabilities.

What is value betting? The basic principle of value betting is best explained by a coin toss. If you rule out that a tossed coin could land on the edge, it will land on the head side with a 50% probability and on the pay side with the same probability. The occurrence of both events is therefore equally likely. Now let's assume that they would have to bet on whether a person rolls head or tails. Fair betting odds would have a value of 2.0. If you bet at these odds, you would have a neutral expectation value, i.e. in the long run you would make neither profit nor loss.

Now they find a bookmaker who offers odds of 2.3 for the result "number is on top". Absolutely you would take the bet, because you know that the real probability of occurrence is 50 % and therefore higher than the one implied in the odds of 2.3, which is 43 % (how to calculate it, see chapter step 2). Statistically there will still be as many numbers as heads up, but you would make a massive profit because on average you would win every second time more than you lost before. If you bet 100 Euro, you get 130 Euro, but only lose 100 Euro.

Professional bettors therefore try to find odds that imply a lower probability than the real probability or the probability assumed by the respective professional sports bettor. Let's take a tennis game between Borna Ćorić and Roger Federer: The odds for a win from Ćorić are 3.3, for a win from Federer 1.39. This means that the bookmaker assumes that Ćorić will only win with a probability of 30 percent. Now a professional bettor analyzes the play and comes to the result that he will win with a probability of 40 per cent. The correct odds should therefore be 2.5! Instead, the bookmaker offers a 3.3. What a mistake! This is therefore a so-called value bet. Probably the favorite, Federer, will win the tennis match, but the professional bets on the outsider because he was wrongly rated. In the long run the professional will make a big profit because of the value.

The fundamental mistake many people make in sports betting is that they see betting as a yes/no decision, like whether team A will win or not. Losers try to recognize the winner. Successful sports bettors, on the other hand, is based on much greater odds.

This explains why it is so difficult to become a profitable sports bettor. Absolute experts with highly professional software calculate the bookmakers' odds. To beat them is only possible if you either have a lot of experience in the sport and have an advantage, insider knowledge or are as experienced in processing statistical information as these experts. Fortunately, there are such private individuals who, fortunately for us, sometimes sell their tips. Nevertheless, before I show you how to find them and how to check their work for seriousness, I would like to briefly explain the work of the bookmakers.

Step 4: Understand the Work of the Bookmakers: The Bookmaker's Margin

The explanation of value betting should have made it clear who our opponent in sports betting is: the bookmakers. They must be beaten. We must be better than them, sound out their weaknesses - namely wrongly set prices, the so-called value bets!

Therefore, it is important that we understand the work of the bookmakers fundamentally. This is one of the most important learning experiences in betting. How do bookmakers earn their money?

I have already explained how to convert odds into probabilities. If you add up all odds probabilities for a bet type of a concrete game, then you get a value that is over 100%. Why is that so?

Let's take the following example from the American basketball league NBA: The game between the Chicago Bulls and the New York Knicks on April 10, 2019. Shortly before the start of the game you would have received the following odds from the online bookmakers Pinnacle and Bwin:

Team	Chicago Bulls	New York Knicks	Sum
Pinnacle Odds	1,83	2,10	-
Probability (100/Quote)	54,64 %	47,62 %	102,26 %
Bwin Odds	1,75	2,10	-
Probability (100/Quote)	57 %	47,62 %	104,62 %

Why is that? The difference between 100% and the sum of the probabilities is the so-called bookmaker's margin, by which the bookmakers make a profit regardless of the outcome of the game. The bookmaker's margin is also known as the commission, or "vig" or "juice".

Let's assume that all tipsters who in Bwin and Pinnacle bet a total of 100,000 Euros on the outcome of the match between the Bulls and Knicks at exactly the mentioned odds with shares proportional to the odds probabilities. This would give the following picture:

PINNACLE	Chicago Bulls	New York Knicks	Sum
Pinnacle Odds	1,83	2,10	-
Set Amount	53.433 Euro	46.567 Euro	100.000 Euro
Win/Loss Victory Chicago Bulls	-44.349 Euro	46.567 Euro	2.218 Euro
Win/Loss Victory New York Knicks	53.433 Euro	-51.224 Euro	2.209 Euro

BWIN	Chicago Bulls	New York Knicks	Sum
Bwin Odds	1,75	2,10	-
Set Amount	54.544 Euro	45.456 Euro	100.000 Euro
Win/Loss Victory Chicago Bulls	-40.908 Euro	45.456 Euro	4.548 Euro
Win/Loss Victory New York Knicks	54.544 Euro	-50.002 Euro	4.542 Euro

In the example for Pinnacle and Bwin it becomes clear that they make a profit regardless of the outcome of the game. Of course, the bookmakers must make a payout according to the winning odds to the customers who bet on the event that occurred. However, by betting on the other outcome of the game, the bookmaker always generates a little more money so that the bookmaker can make a profit regardless of the outcome of the game. This is the so-called bookmaker's margin.

Let us clarify the principle once again using the example of a coin toss bet. Let's assume a constant bet of 10 Euro. The event you can bet on is either head or tails, with a 50% probability of occurrence. The "fair" odds would therefore be 2.0. Person A bets on head, person B on number. No matter who wins, the bookmaker would have to pay 20 Euro (bet plus win) for every coin toss. This means that he would have to pay out as much as he would take from the lost bet of the other customer and thus never make a profit. That would not be a good business model. For this reason, every bookmaker reduces the odds by a few percent. So instead of offering "fair" odds of 2.0 on a coin toss, a bookmaker would choose odds of 1.9, for example. No matter which event now occurs, he would have to pay out 19 euros to one person, retain the stake of 10 euros from the other person, and thus make a profit of 1 euro with each coin toss.

For you as a bettor, this means that blind betting, i.e. without paying attention to the expected value of a bet, will lose on average a percentage of your money corresponding to the margin. If a bookmaker's margin is 4.5 percent, you would lose 4.5 cents on average for every blindly placed euro.

The challenge for a sports weather that wants to be successful in the long run is to find a quota that is so high that it compensates for the bookmaker's margin and also promises a positive expected value: If a bookmaker were to misjudge the probability of the coin being flipped and grant a quota of 2.2 on the event, then one would have an expected value and one should place the bet accordingly. Perhaps one loss in the short term because the probability of occurrence is "only" 50 % for every coin toss, but statistically one would have an advantage over the bookmaker in every round and would therefore make a profit in the long term.

Step 5: Find Profitable Tipsters Based on the Right Criteria and Unmask Fraudsters

The Beating of the Closing Line

Success or failure in the betting business depends on whether a tipster can reliably filter out bets with value from the wide range on offer. But how does one know afterwards whether a bet placed has had value? In the long run, the success of a bet is of course measured by whether your own betting bank is constantly growing or whether you are constantly making a loss. But we don't want to risk replaying the worthless bets of fraudulent tipsters and can therefore check in advance whether it is worth investing in a tip seller. There is a powerful method for this, which will be presented in the following.

It was already explained that the odds are subject to strong fluctuations up to the play beginning. This is caused by the new information in the form of money flows and news about player injuries etc. that hit the market. This makes the odds so efficient that the closing rate of the bookmaker Pinnacle.com, which converts very high bet amounts, represents 99% (!) of the actual probability distribution. If the closing line at Pinnacle, for example, is 2.0, then the probability of occurrence of the relevant betting event is 50 percent. The closing rate is therefore a measure with which you can check afterwards whether bets had value. For example, if the last odds offered by Pinnacle on the victory of the Chicago Bulls are 1.6, but you took a 1.75, then you can assume with a high probability that you bet with Value. If you succeed often enough in taking such value bets, then you are on the road to success.

Due to the included random variance in the prediction of game results, no sports bettor can beat the closing line all the time. Even though the predictions are well-founded, the influence of suddenly announced player injuries, changes in the team line-up and other random events cannot be predicted, so the expected value can slip into the negative. However, the only decisive factor is whether the closing line is beaten often enough by a tipster and whether he can record a positive expectation value when looking at a larger number of his recommended bets.

But how do you calculate the expected value? First, the margin of the bookmaker must be deducted from the closing line in order to obtain the actual "fair" odds. Every bookmaker estimates different margins. The so-called "Asian bookmakers" like Pinnacle, SBO and 188Bet take comparatively very small margins (see chapter "Step 7"). They have the most efficient odds, so European bookmakers such as Tipico, Bwin and Interwetten follow them. If the odds of Asian bookmakers rise or fall, this fluctuation is also reflected with a time lag in European betting providers. The Asian markets are very popular with professional bettors not only because of the low margin, but also because they accept high stakes - not least because of the larger money flows, the odds of Asian bookmakers are only so efficient (remember the market law: money = information).

You calculate the margin as follows: (100/quota option A) + (100/quota option B). Let's take as an example an encounter between the Toronto Raptors and the Golden State Warriors in the American Basketball League NBA on 31.05.2019. For a victory of the Raptors you got a quota of 1.84 at Pinnacle, for a defeat a quota of 2.08. This results in a ratio of 1.84 for a victory of the Raptors:

$$((100/1.84) + (100/2.08)) - 100 = 2.43 \text{ percent}$$

The bookmaker Pinnacle's margin he had set for this game was 2.43 percent. On the website Oddsportal.com, you can compare the odds of different bookmakers for a wide range of tournaments for free. It is also automatically shown what margin each bookmaker takes.

The expected value of a bet, less the margin, must be positive for it to be a Value Bet. The goal is therefore to beat the margin-adjusted closing line. But how is the expected value calculated at all? Pinnacle's closing odds will simply be divided by the odds bet and multiplied by 100. If you have bet odds of 1.9 and the final odds are 1.8, you get: (1.9/1.8) x 100 = 5.56 percent. The bet had a positive expected value of 5.56 percent. The margin must be subtracted from this, which is 2.5 %, for example, so that the margin-adjusted expected value is 3.06 percent. In other words: For every euro you bet on such a bet, you will make a profit of 3.06 cents in the long run! Of course, you must consider the variance: 10 bets can be lost in a row. Such streaks of bad luck happen but should not worry as long as you reliably beat the margin-free closing line. As the number of bets increases, the variance decreases. That's why I said at the beginning of the book that luck only determines skill in the short term, skill in the long term!

By comparing the quote taken with the closing line, we have learned an effective method of checking the profitability of a tipster. In the following chapter, this parameter is supplemented by further criteria.

Criteria for the Selection of a Tipster

Serious Tipster Services should help you get insight into their balance sheet. If they don't, you should stay away automatically, as the provider's work cannot be checked. The statistics must contain the following information: Information about the bets placed (date of the match, teams or players for individual sports), the odds typed, the bet type, which bookmaker the bet was placed with, whether it was won or lost and an indication of the monthly and total return earned.

The first step of the check requires a bit of self-work, but it is worth it: First you write down all your bets in a table for a certain time period. The Microsoft Excel program, for example, is suitable for this. The more bets you place, the more meaningful your statistics will be. Then compare the odds taken from the tipster with the margin-free closing line, which you can research on oddsportal.com, for example. Five table columns are required. In the first column you note the date on which the game took place. In the second column you write the players or teams. In the third you note the odds taken from the tipster, in the fourth you note the margin-free closing line. In the fifth column you enter the expected value, which can be either negative or positive. Once this is complete, mark the entire fifth column and add all the expected values. In Microsoft Excel this can be done automatically by the sum function and you save some time. If the average value calculated in this way is in the positive range, then this means that the tipster will make a long-term profit corresponding to the average value with his betting behavior. If, for example, the expected value is 5 percent, then you win 5 cents for every euro you invest in the tipster's bets.

If you take a closer look at a Tipster service, you should not only use the statistics to check whether the player manages to beat the margin-free closing line reliably and what the expected value is. Although this is the central tool for the evaluation of a tipster, you should also clarify the following questions:

What Yield Can the Tipster Show?

In sports betting, the yield generated by a tipster is usually referred to by the English term "yield". The yield indicates the effectiveness of betting. If a bettor has a monthly turnover of 10,000 Euros, i.e. has placed this sum on its individual bets and at the end of the month 9,000 Euros remain in the betting bank, then it unfortunately has a negative yield of -10 percent. Conversely, with a result of 11,000 euros, he would have made a profit of 1,000 euros and thus earned a yield of 10 percent.

The net profit is calculated by subtracting the bet amount from the winning amount:

Win amount - Bet amount = Net profit

Formula: [(Win Sum - Bet Total) / Bet Total] x 100%

It's very hard to beat the Asian bookers. Any positive yield on a larger number of bets is therefore a good performance. A yield in the range of four to 15 percent is excellent. A yield of over 15 percent will not hold a tipster in the long run. So, you should be skeptical if a service with such a balance advertises itself.

Does the Tipster Offer Combination Bets or Only Single Bets?

Professional sports betting concentrates on single bets and only makes combination bets in certain cases. The odds increase with the combination, but the probability that the bet will be won decreases proportionally. Although in the long run it makes no difference whether you play single or combination bets, as the value of a value bet also multiplies, the variance becomes much greater. In the balance sheet, there is significantly greater volatility. In order to avoid the risk of longer "streaks of bad luck", you should therefore only place individual bets. Only odds that are so low that a very high amount would have to be bet in order to realize the target profit can be included in a double bet. Apart from that, there is no reason to play combination bets. They belong in the realm of fun bets. Tipster services that offer combination bets are aimed at these fun bets and are usually not serious.

Which Sports and Competitions or Leagues Does the Tipster Focus on?

Reliably recognizing value in the sports betting market requires a strong specialization in certain sports, if not leagues. One rule is therefore that you should only trust tipsters who concentrate on one sport, or better still on certain leagues or competitions. A tipster who plays everything from badminton to football to Formula 1 is either a genius or, more likely, a fraud.

It's easier to find Value in smaller competitions that are not so much the focus of bookmakers like the English Premiere League or the Spanish La Liga. The same applies to less popular sports such as sailing or volleyball. This may sound good at first, but it has one disadvantage: bookmakers do not allow very large amounts in smaller competitions. If you're just setting up your betting bank and are only betting double-digit amounts, then this shouldn't be particularly disadvantageous for you. But if you want to play larger stakes with increasing capital growth, then it's quite limiting.

Another disadvantage is the comparison of the tipster odds with the closing line. In small competitions the closing line is not so meaningful. Even if the closing odds are not beaten, a bet can still contain value. It has already been stated that money in the sports betting market corresponds to information. Therefore, the odds in competitions in which large money flows (high-liquidity markets) are much more efficient. In small markets (low-liquidity markets), on the other hand, even individual high stakes can noticeably change the odds.

You should have tipsters that concentrate on niche sports or niche leagues in your portfolio! With increasing capital investment, however, they are more than additions to the portfolio, because they can be "driving forces".

Which Bookmakers Does the Tipster Use?

Only choose Tipsters that place bets exclusively with Asian bookmakers! European bookmakers sometimes have higher odds, but the European bookmakers quickly limit especially customers who can reliably make profits. Then it is only permitted to bet relatively small stakes, which are too small to even earn the price for the Tipster Service. These bookmakers will even look specifically for whether you are betting on Value and limit you if necessary, because they know that they would lose against Value-Tippers in the long run.

Asian bookmakers behave very differently here. They welcome value bettors because their goal is to generate the most efficient odds possible. As I said earlier, Asian bookmakers are also targeting smaller margins, so the odds are higher on average.

Another decisive advantage of Asian bookmakers is that they do not collect betting tax. European bookmakers levy the German betting tax of five percent for German customers. Some levy this tax on the stake, most on the profit plus the stake, i.e. on the turnover. The betting tax reduces the value of a bet to such an extent that the respective tipster service would have to generate a very high yield for the betting to be worthwhile.

Therefore, you can immediately sort out all tipsters that include European bookmakers in their bets. The European bookmakers have on average lower odds, but also more often odds slip upwards. So, it is much easier to beat European bookmakers than Asian bookmakers. To have a high yield with European bookmakers is therefore not as impressive as beating a bookmaker like Pinnacle in the long run. Search for bettors, which concentrate on the Asiatic markets, because only those are genuine professionals!

How Many Bets Has the Tipster Already Placed?

Short-term strands of bad luck or luck have no significance over the ability of a tipster. Only those who can make a profit on a large number of bets can play in the king's class. Therefore, when choosing a Tipster service, you should concentrate on those providers who already have more than 1000 tips. These bets should all be verifiable in the statistics. A tipster who does not reveal all his bets has something to hide! Of course, there are also the "rising stars" among the tipsters, who can only show a smaller number of verified tips. If such a candidate can only show 50 tips, but clearly beats the closing line, he can be quite interesting. But it takes a lot of time to filter out the young talents from the large number of tipsters that have short-term success. It is therefore more timesaving to make a preselection based on the number of tips already submitted - no tipsters with less than 1,000 tips!

What Is the Service Price?

Just like you, Tipster services want to earn money. That's their right, because in return they let you share their knowledge. Skepticism is more in demand when it comes to supposedly free or low-price offers.

Some tipsters offer monthly subscriptions, others pay per tip. For providers with monthly subscription fees, you should check how many tips the service gives on average per month and convert this number to the individual tip price. This makes the comparison easier.

In order to decide whether a Tipster service is profitable for you in terms of price, you should first determine which stake you can make per bet (see also step 9). Multiply the number of bets by the stake and the average yield of the tipster. Now you have the expected profit and can compare it with the cost. If you subtract the costs from the expected profit, then you have your net profit as a result. This value should of course be positive. Here you can see that it is necessary to have a sufficiently large betting bank to be able to bet profitably.

Is There Background Information About the Tipster?

In addition to the criteria already described, you should find out who is behind the service. Serious tipsters have a description of their own biography. Which competences qualify him? Does the information sound plausible? A tipster who does not explain his career in a comprehensible way should be viewed with skepticism. A serious sports bettor usually has many years of experience in the business, has sound knowledge of IT and statistics and is intensively informed about news about games taking place, which he includes in his probability calculation.

In Concrete Terms: Set Off in Search of Profitable Tipsters!

Of course, you are now asking yourself where to research for serious tipsters in order to implement the knowledge you have learned. There are various platforms on the

Internet where sports bettors sell their tips. These include pyckio.com, betadvisor.com and inbetsment.com. The advantages of these portals are that they provide extensive statistics about the tipsters. Based on these values you can come to a well-founded assessment of the respective tipsters. Even the individual bets of the past are listed, and the odds taken are indicated, so that a retrospective comparison with the final odds is possible and you can calculate the expected value for each sports bet as described. You can also have the balance of the tipster displayed for each month. Even with very successful tipsters, you will discover months in which he has finished in the minus. This is due to the statistical variance. Bets with a positive expected value can also be lost. With successful sports bettors there are months of loss, but never a year of loss!

Step 6: Diversification: Reduce Risk by Creating a Broad Tipster Portfolio

Since even profitable tipsters can have a streak of bad luck, it is better not to rely solely on sports bettors. The risk of loss can be minimized by investing in diversification, as with an equity portfolio. As you know, every equity professional does not only have share certificates from a single company in his portfolio, because if this one company were to lose in the market, the investor would lose a lot of money! Instead, you spread your capital over several companies, which greatly reduces the risk of a total loss.

The same applies to betting. Choose several tipsters and buy tips from them. This will also increase your monthly betting volume and increase your turnover. When making your selection, you should make sure that the Tipsters concentrate on different sports and leagues. For example, choose a football specialist who focuses on the Spanish leagues and another who bets on English football. Then there's a basketball tipster and pros who focus on tennis, volleyball and other sports. With such a broad line-up, the losses one tipster makes in a losing streak are offset by the profits of the others.

Of course, you should check at regular intervals whether your tipsters are still on the right path and continue to beat the closing line reliably. If they don't, throw them out of your portfolio and replace them with more profitable providers.

Step 7: Place Your Bets With the Right Bookmakers

Place your bets with the Asian bookies. These are among others:

- Pinnacle

- IBC Bet

- SBOBET

- SINGBET

- BETISN

- GA288 (GALAXY BET)

These bookmakers take the lowest margins compared to European bookmakers like Tipico, Bet365 or Bwin, allow the highest stakes and do not limit successful players! Professional Tipster services only offer tips for these bookmakers, so you'll never have to decide anyway. For German customers, the 5 percent betting tax collected by the European bookmakers would also reduce your yield to such an extent that it would be much more difficult to make a profit in the long run.

Nevertheless, it should be mentioned that there are also European bookmakers who waive the collection of the betting tax and pay it out of their own pockets to the tax authorities in order to be more attractive to customers. These are:

- 1XBET

- 5dimes

- 32red

- BetfairSB

- Betfirst

- Expekt

- Guts

- Intertops

- Leonbets

- PlanetWin365

- Tipico

- Titanbet

There's nothing wrong with involving these bookies. Mostly the Asian bookmakers will offer the highest odds, but it can also happen that you discover higher odds with a European bookmaker who is exempt from betting tax. If they haven't limited you yet, you can "cup" these bookies. The bookmakers offer a bonus on your first deposit. Especially when you are in the process of setting up a betting bank, it can be advantageous to unlock the bonuses of the European bookmakers. For example, Tipico doubles your first deposit. However, you must wager this amount three times. If you deposit 100 Euros, then you have 200 on your betting account at Tipico, but you can only withdraw this additional money if you have bet it three times in a certain period. However, if you do not meet the conditions in a given period, the bonus will be forfeited.

But let's turn back to Asian bookmakers. In the hunt for the highest odds, there is a big help: platforms like sportmarket.com, betinasia.com and asianodds88.com allow us to open an account, where you can play different Asian bookmakers at the same time. As with other bookmakers, the games you can bet on are displayed. You can then decide for each game which bookmaker you want to bet on. As you will see all available odds for the game, you can choose the highest odds currently available on the market.

Whether you take odds of 1.73 or 1.76 may seem marginal to you, but in the long run there is a clear difference in the betting bank. In addition to the advantage of always being able to see and select the best odds at a glance, you will be relieved of work by not having to open an account with every bookmaker separately. This saves time and you don't have to spread your capital across multiple betting accounts.

Step 8: Be Time-Efficient: Automated Betting

The tipsters in your portfolio will publish their tips at different times. They will send you an email with all the information you need about the bet. Especially if you follow several tipsters and play several hundred bets every month, you would have to be constantly on your PC or smartphone to read the incoming e-mails and place your bets. It's not effective to just want to do this at a certain time of day, because you can't wait too long to place a bet. If your Tipster offers value beds, it means, as mentioned earlier, that it has discovered inefficient odds in the market. Since the odds in the market are constantly fluctuating and weak points are quickly balanced out, you must be quick to get the value odds. To save yourself this stress, software has been developed that automatically reads the tipster emails you receive and places the recommended bets. You can, of course, choose which bets you want to play with. One of the best software of this kind is Smartbet.io. The price is related to your bets and is 0.25 percent of your bet in automated betting. So that you don't have to run your PC all the time for the software to work, you can set up a virtual PC that costs 0.50 EUR per 24 hours. The software can be connected to platforms like sportmarket.com or asianodds88.com.

Step 9: Ensure Healthy Capital and Risk Management

As with the stock market, one should be aware of the risks and only invest money whose loss would not entail existential hardships. Never bet money that you could not do without! In the long run, sports betting promises impressive profits, but in the short run you can also lose a lot of money.

In order to reduce the risk, you should draw up a plan for calculating the stakes, which you must adhere to in a disciplined manner. Do not increase the stakes to recoup lost money. This could accelerate the downward trend. Instead, trust the value of the bets or the positive expected value, which you can always check by comparing the odds with the closing line.

What is the best way to calculate your bet amount? Many sports bettors swear by the Kelly criterion, which calculates your bet in relation to the odds and the value it promises. The greater the assumed value, the higher the stake according to this method. You can find the corresponding calculators free of charge on the Internet. The disadvantage of this type of bet calculation, however, is that it is initially only a presumed value. Nobody can be sure where the final quota will end up. Therefore, when calculating the stakes using the Kelly criterion, it can quickly happen that you invest too much capital.

Therefore, two other methods are recommended here:

I. The first method is the fixed bet method. For each bet, you bet a predetermined amount, regardless of the odds or the value of the bet. This should never be more than two percent of your betting bank. The bigger your betting bank is, the stronger your bet should move in the direction of 0.5 percent.

II. The second method works with a target profit that you set for the bets. This should never be more than one percent of the betting capital. If your betting bank has an amount of 10,000 EUR, then your target profit would be 100 EUR, for example. Subtract a one from the respective odds and divide the target profit by this value. In this way you calculate the stake for each set of odds:

Example: odds: 1.7 - 1 = 0.7 100 EUR / 0.7 = 142.86 EUR stake

Betting with a target profit has the advantage that you bet roughly proportional to the risk. Bets with high odds will of course be lost more often than bets with small odds. By calculating a target profit, high odds are proportionally bet on small amounts so that the risk is minimized. The disadvantage is that you would have to bet very high for very low odds. Therefore, you should never bet more than two percent of your capital.

Not all automated betting software offers the ability to calculate bets based on the target profit. If you want to save time and effort, you should therefore choose betting with fixed stakes.

End

This book has given you the knowledge you need to know whether a Tipster service is a promising provider or a fraudulent rip-off. Perhaps the book has opened your eyes to the immense return opportunities available to everyone in the sports betting market. Conventional investment products cannot keep up here.

Contrary to the promises of other guidebook literature to the topic sport bets, here not the illusion was sold that everyone can find the correct bets over night with a few simple tricks or strategies. Instead, you should let the real professionals do the work for you and profit from their skills.

A relatively small expenditure with the search for very good Tipsters faces a substantial chance on rich net yield. If one selects the correct offerers wisely, then one is on a good way to passive income.

There will certainly also be months in which you have a negative balance, but if the tipsters in your portfolio reliably beat the margin-free closing line, you can sit back and relax. Because you know: Happiness only decides success in the short term, ability decides in the long term!

Further Links

Important bookies:

https://bet-ibc.com/de/

https://www.pinnacle.com

https://www.sbobet.com

A platform for placing sports bets where you can choose between several bookmakers to get the best odds:

https://www.asianodds88.com

Platforms for providers of betting tips. Here you can buy tips from real professionals:

https://www.betadvisor.com/de

https://www.inbetsment.com

https://pyckio.com/

A tool to automate the process of placing your bets:

https://smartbet.io/

https://www.oddsportal.com/

This is a site where you can compare the odds of different bookmakers for a variety of games. Under "Archived Results" you can find the closing odds of past encounters.

Made in the USA
Coppell, TX
28 November 2020